THE NEW CREEPY CRAWLY COLLECTION

DRAGONFLIES

For a free color catalog describing Gareth Stevens' list of high-quality books and multimedia programs, call 1-800-542-2595 (USA) or 1-800-461-9120 (Canada). Gareth Stevens Publishing's Fax: (414) 225-0377. See our catalog, too, on the World Wide Web: http://gsinc.com

Library of Congress Cataloging-in-Publication Data

Amery, Heather.
    Dragonflies / by Heather Amery ; illustrated by Tony Gibbons.
      p. cm. -- (The New creepy crawly collection)
    Includes bibliographical references (p. 24) and index.
    Summary: Describes the physical characteristics, life cycle, and behavior of dragonflies, as well as miscellaneous facts about these swift flying insects.
    ISBN 0-8368-1579-3 (lib. bdg.)
    1. Dragonflies--Juvenile literature. [1. Dragonflies.] I. Gibbons, Tony, ill. II. Title. III. Series.
QL520.A54 1996
595.7'33--dc20   95-54173

This North American edition first published in 1996 by
Gareth Stevens Publishing
1555 North RiverCenter Drive, Suite 201
Milwaukee, Wisconsin 53212 USA

This U.S. edition © 1996 by Gareth Stevens, Inc. Created with original © 1995 by Quartz Editorial Services, 112 Station Road, Edgware HA8 7AQ U.K.

Additional illustrations by Clare Heronneau.

Consultant: Matthew Robertson, Senior Keeper, Bristol Zoo, Bristol, England.

Printed in Mexico

1 2 3 4 5 6 7 8 9 99 98 97 96

THE NEW

CREEPY CRAWLY

COLLECTION

DRAGONFLIES

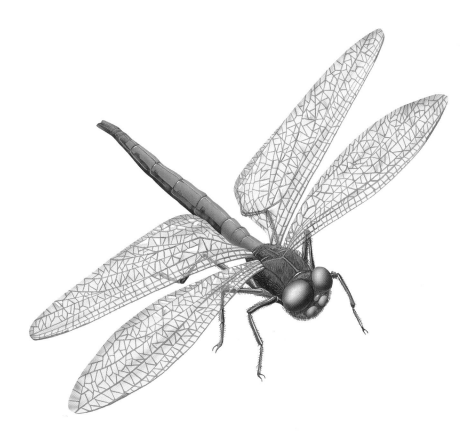

by Heather Amery

Illustrated by Tony Gibbons

Gareth Stevens Publishing

MILWAUKEE

Contents

Getting to know
dragonflies

Quick as a flash, something blue or green darts across a stream or a pond. It could be a dragonfly, one of the fastest of all the flying insects.

There are over 5,000 different kinds of dragonflies, and they have been around for over 300 million years. This means they existed

long before there were any birds, or even pterodactyls, flying around in the sky. And they were once much larger than any dragonfly you will see on Earth today.

What sort of environment do dragonflies like? How long do they live? Is it true they can fly backward and turn somersaults? What do they eat? How do they mate? Join us on a dragonfly safari and find out all about these fascinating and colorful insects.

Colorful

The dragonfly's most obvious feature is its beautiful wings. It has two pairs, with a dark mark on the tip of each. They are very thin and gauzelike, with a pattern of fine veins that help keep them stiff. Even when resting, dragonflies have their wings outspread.

Different kinds of dragonflies have different patterns on their wings. Many also have bright blue or green bodies, but some are red or orange; a few have black and yellow stripes.

A dragonfly has a fairly large head, which it can turn around in almost all directions. At the front are two huge eyes, and there are three extra small ones at the top. Below the eyes are two jaws with sawlike teeth.

The dragonfly's scientific name, *Odonata*, means "toothed creature." It also has two tiny antennae for touching and smelling. You may not notice them because they can be thin and almost invisible.

6

creatures

A dragonfly's long, thin body has two main parts. The thorax houses its wing muscles. Its six legs, joined to this part of its body, are thin and covered with bristles. It uses them to cling to a plant when resting.

Its legs are not much use for walking, but are useful for catching prey.

The second part of a dragonfly's body is the abdomen, which contains the stomach and breathing equipment. It doesn't have lungs, but it does have thin tubes that take in air and carry it around the body. At the end of the abdomen are two pincers, or claspers, which a male dragonfly uses to grasp a female when mating.

During daylight hours, you will rarely see a dragonfly sitting still for more than a few seconds. If you do spot one, by the time you count to twenty it will probably be in the air again, hovering, diving, or swerving this way and that. Dragonflies can also fly for long distances — hundreds of miles (kilometers) — at a time.

Dragonflies move through the air so efficiently that an early type of French airplane was named after them. It was called the *Demoiselle* (DEM-WAH-ZELL), which is the French word for a type of dragonfly.

Life

An adult dragonfly may live for only about two weeks. Even the longest-living die after about six weeks. But this is only one stage of its life.

Then it selects a female and tries to grab her head or body with its legs. If the female is willing, they fly off together to mate.

When a male dragonfly is ready to mate, it wanders around a watery place for a week or so. It spends its time marking off some territory as its own and driving away any rival males.

The female soon lays her eggs on water weeds in mud or in water, and flies away. Different kinds of dragonflies lay their eggs in different places. The eggs usually hatch two to five weeks after being laid.

cycle

When the larva, or nymph, comes out of the egg, it lives under the water at first. The wingless nymph can breathe under water through special organs known as gills. But it cannot see well yet, and will stay in the water, eating hungrily, for up to two years.

When the nymph is fully grown, it crawls up the stem of a plant until it is out of the water and hangs there. Amazingly, the nymph's skin now gradually splits, so its head and body can break free.

During its nymph stage — much longer than its adult life — it will shed its skin as many as fifteen times.

The creature that emerges is a fully grown dragonfly.

In flight

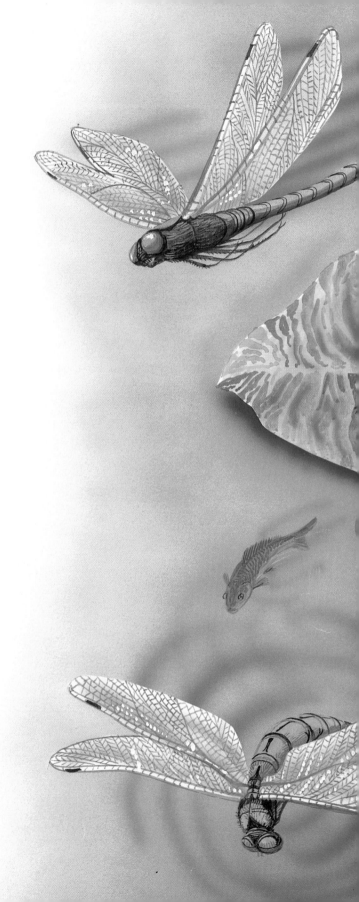

Dragonflies can fly faster than almost any other insect. Some scientists think they can even reach speeds of up to 65 miles (104 km) per hour over short distances. It is very difficult, however, to measure accurately the speed of an insect that flies so quickly.

Dragonflies can hover, dart, turn somersaults in the air, and fly backward at great speed. At their fastest, their wings beat up to thirty times a second. Dragonflies even rest with their wings open. Their close relatives, the damselflies, will perch with their wings folded over their backs.

Their flying speed and acrobatics help dragonflies escape from most predators that chase them for a tasty meal. Their agility in the air also helps dragonflies catch their own insect prey. Some will even swoop swiftly to grab tadpoles or small fish.

Looking

Dragonflies have large, bulging eyes that may be bright blue, green, or red. With these eyes, they can see almost all around — even behind their heads. And they can spot a meal, such as the fly in this illustration, that is in flight as far as 40 feet (12 meters) away.

A dragonfly's eyes, known as compound eyes, seem to cover almost its entire head. Each eye is made up of thirty thousand different six-sided parts. Because all the parts are set at different angles, each has a slightly different view of the world.

Each part of a compound eye has a lens, or facet, giving the dragonfly's brain as many as thirty thousand slightly different tiny images. These are then made into a single picture of what the dragonfly sees.

at you

The image the dragonfly sees is probably not as clear as the picture we see when we look at the same thing. But a dragonfly's compound eyes are excellent in other ways. They are useful, for example, for looking in all directions and for detecting small movements. Being able to swivel their heads also helps dragonflies see all around them.

It is good that dragonflies are able to see well because their antennae, which they use for touching and smelling, are not very well developed. This is why dragonflies are most active during the daytime hours, when it is light outdoors, and rest at night, when it is dark.

The dragonfly diet

Dragonflies are wonderful hunters. Because they fly so fast and are so acrobatic, they can catch most other insects in the air. Using their legs like a basket to trap prey, they will take a large insect back to a favorite perch and eat it there. Large dragonflies may even swoop down over water to grab a small frog or fish. The dragonfly shown here has caught a small dobson fly. All dragonflies are carnivores, which means they eat other living animals, not plants.

When a dragonfly has hatched out of its egg as a nymph and starts to live in the water, it eats enormous amounts of food. Anything that happens to come within range — such as other insect larvae, water lice, worms, tadpoles, and small fish — will be snapped up in its powerful jaws.

But once a dragonfly nymph emerges from its watery home and splits out of its skin, it is in great danger. Unable to fly for an hour or two, it may itself be eaten by spiders, fish, or waterbirds.

Many birds would like to make a meal of an adult dragonfly, but few are swift and agile enough to catch one. The exception is a type of hawk called a falcon. This bird of prey can fly faster than dragonflies and hunts them down, catching them in the air.

Water-loving

The best place to spot dragonflies is near water. Although some dragonflies fly in summer through open woodlands and rest in the sun on bushes, they all mate in watery places. The females then lay their eggs in water. A large pond with clean water may sometimes be a home for as many as six different dragonfly species. Some skim low through the reeds, while others patrol backward and forward, several feet (m) above open water. Some dragonflies seem to prefer boggy pools where the water is dark and acidic. Others seek out fast-flowing mountain streams, stagnant ponds or lakes, broad

insects

rivers, or canals. No one knows for certain why dragonflies choose to live by one kind of water rather than another. But when a dragonfly visits water for the first time, it often touches the water with its abdomen. This may be to check that it is not just a puddle that might dry up in the sun. Whichever type of watery place a dragonfly selects, it likes one with some pond weeds, reeds, or other plants growing along the banks. It uses the reeds and plants as resting perches. The dragonfly nymphs will crawl up these plants when they emerge from the water, ready to turn into adult dragonflies.

Myths and

Dragonflies are known by a variety of popular names as a result of the ancient beliefs and legends surrounding them. Dragonflies with long, thin bodies, for instance, were once called "devil's darning needles" because of a superstition that dragonflies sew up the eyes, noses, mouths, and ears of people, especially children, when they are asleep. This, of course, is not true!

The name "horse-stinger" probably comes from the dragonfly's habit of flying around these animals. When horses graze near water on a warm, summer day, they are often surrounded by clouds of flies. These naturally attract dragonflies, which are in search of an easy meal. But dragonflies do not actually sting any living creature. Dragonflies are also called "mosquito hawks." They are not related to mosquitoes, however, and probably only got the name "hawk" because, like this bird, they are good hunters and fast fliers.

legends

Another common name for dragonflies is "snake-feeder." Dragonflies got this name because people thought, quite wrongly, that they attacked snakes and other types of reptiles.

Many other superstitions are also associated with dragonflies. In the United States, for example, some people once feared that, if someone killed a dragonfly, a member of his or her family would die. In Britain, people once believed that a dragonfly would lead a good boy to a place where he could catch lots of fish. Naughty boys would be led to places where there were no fish.

In Japan, dragonflies were once believed to be very lucky. Warriors even carried them into battle to bring victory, and they were symbols of courage and manliness. The country of Japan also bears the name *Akitsushima*, which means "land of the dragonflies."

True dragonflies

Not all insects that look like dragonflies *are* dragonflies. True dragonflies usually have thick bodies, and their large eyes almost meet on the front of their heads. True dragonflies are divided into two types — hawkers and darters. Hawkers get their name from their habit of patrolling up and down a stretch of water or countryside.

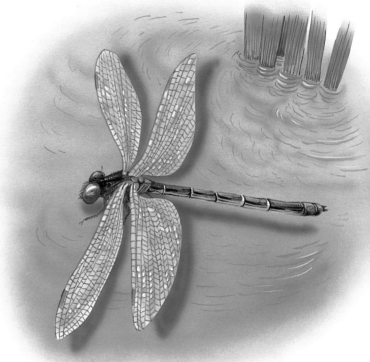

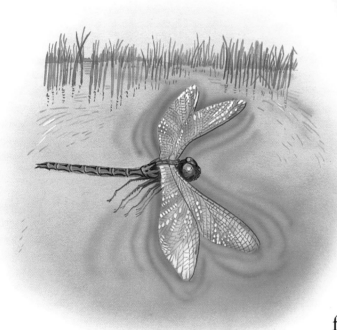

Hawkers will fly for hours, usually several feet (m) above the ground, searching for food or looking for a mate. Darters prefer to choose a dry reed or stick, and settle there, warming themselves in the sun. They will then suddenly dart from their perches to catch food in the air or to chase away rivals — which is how they get their name.

or damselflies?

Damselflies are usually smaller than true dragonflies, with thin, delicate bodies, and eyes on the sides of their heads. Damselflies are not strong fliers. Instead, they flutter through the reeds or skim along just above the water. They seldom fly far from their watery breeding grounds. When resting, damselflies usually fold their wings over their backs.

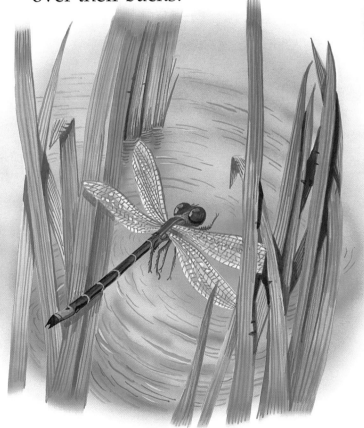

Both true dragonflies and damselflies get their common names either from their coloring or from the way they behave; for example, the blue-tailed damselfly, red-eyed damselfly, white-faced darter, and azure hawker. Can you identify each of those shown here? These are just four of over five thousand dragonfly varieties.

21

Did you know?

How many kinds of dragonflies are there?
There are over five thousand different kinds of dragonflies. A few have become extinct in the last fifty years, but new ones have also been recorded and assigned names. Many more may still be waiting to be discovered.

▲ Are any dragonflies dangerous?
Although adult dragonflies have large jaws and pincers at the ends of their bodies, they rarely bite. They are dangerous only to other insects, which they eat in large quantities. Dragonfly nymphs, as shown above, bite more often, however, and can give a nasty nip.

Are they found all over the world?
Dragonflies live in all parts of the world that have water, warm weather, and plenty of food. They cannot survive in very cold climates. The largest number of species are found in the tropics.

▼ What is their biggest wingspan?
The largest dragonfly living today has a wingspan of over 7 inches (19 centimeters). But dragonflies that zoomed around millions of years ago had wingspans up to 30 inches (75 cm).

▲ Do dragonflies have enemies?

Birds are the main predators of dragonflies, particularly falcons and swallows. A spider's web can also be a dangerous trap, as you can see in the illustration above. Sometimes, too, one species of dragonfly will attack another.

Which are the largest and smallest dragonflies?

The largest dragonfly has a wingspan that is a little longer than your hand and a body just half this length. It lives in South America. The smallest lives in Myanmar (Burma) and has a wingspan and body that are each only about the size of your middle fingernail.

Are dragonflies intelligent?

Although dragonflies have large heads, most of the space is taken up with large eyes and jaws. There is not a lot of room for brains. They behave by instinct rather than by thinking, as humans do.

Are they useful in any way?

Dragonflies are useful because they eat other insects that bite, sting, and spread diseases, such as mosquitoes. One dragonfly can eat its own body weight in just thirty minutes! Just imagine eating a meal that weighed as much as you do! Humans would get very ill if they tried this.

▼ *Are all dragonflies brightly colored?*

Most dragonflies have brilliantly colored wings and bodies, but the males usually have the brightest colors. The dragonfly's body coloring develops slowly after the adult dragonfly has emerged from its nymph stage. In some dragonfly species, the color fades as the dragonfly dies.

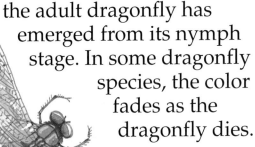

Glossary

antennae — movable sensory organs on an insect's head that are used for touching and smelling.

carnivores — meat-eaters.

compound eye — an eye made up of many lenses. The dragonfly's compound eyes have thousands of lenses that receive many images, which the brain then interprets as one picture.

facet — the flat surface of a lens within the eye.

gills — organs that take in oxygen from the water for breathing.

larva — the wingless stage of an insect's life between the egg and the pupa.

lens — the part of the eye used to focus light rays.

predators — animals that hunt and kill other animals for food.

prey — animals that are killed by other animals for food.

thorax — the chest cavity, which houses the heart and lungs. The thorax is the middle section of an insect's body.

Books and Videos

Dragonflies. James P. Rowan (Rourke)

Dragonfly. Emery Bernhard (Holiday House)

Dragonfly. Barrie Watts (Silver Burdett)

The World of Dragonflies. Virginia Harrison (Gareth Stevens)

The Dragonfly. (Barr Films video)

See How They Grow Pond Animals. Dorling Kindersley video (Sony Wonder)

Index